Emmett's Vacuums

Written and photographed by Tracy Cronce

Published by:
Beckham Publications, Inc.

Text copyright © 2018 Tracy Cronce
Photos copyright © 2018 Tracy Cronce

All rights reserved. No part of this publication may be reproduced or transmitted in any form or by any means, electronic or mechanical, including photocopying, recording, taping or any information storage and retrieval system, without permission in writing from Beckham Publications, Inc.

ISBN ISBN-13: 978-1986663977

ISBN-10: 1986663973

This is Emmett.

Emmett really likes vacuums.

This is a Dirt Devil vacuum.

The Dirt Devil is a bagless vacuum.

The Dirt Devil has a beater bar.

The beater bar has bristles.

Bristles help to pick up dirt.

Toy vacuums are fun to play with.

Many toy vacuums run on a battery.

This vacuum has a hose to get to small spots.

Look at the handheld vacuum that Emmett has. It is lightweight.

After vacuuming, Emmett can empty the dust bin.

This toy vacuum also has a beater bar.

Green wheels help the vacuum to roll on the floor.

Hoover makes a full size bagless vacuum.

When the canister is full, Emmett will empty it.

Attachments like these extension wands are parts of the vacuum that help to clean small spots.

The extension wand clips into place on the vacuum's side. A stretchy hose helps Emmett to clean hard-to-reach places.

To turn on the Hoover vacuum, Emmett plugs in the vacuum and then uses his foot to push the lever.

Bristles cover the beater bar on this Hoover vacuum.

Shop-Vacs are vacuums that can clean up both wet and dry areas. This Shop-Vac is chrome colored. It also has a long black hose with a floor brush attachment.

With the push of a button, the Shop-Vac will open up.

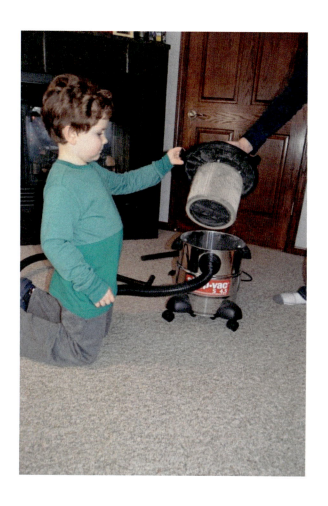

Inside the Shop-Vac you will find a round filter.

A large drum on the inside holds everything the Shop-Vac sucks up. It is easy to empty.

Eureka is the name of this bagless vacuum.

A long hose with a wand attachment are on the back of the Eureka.

This bagless vacuum also needs to be emptied when it's full.

The red button will turn on the vacuum after it's plugged in.

Here Emmett is showing the yellow bristles on the beater bar of the Eureka.

Look at the little red Shop-Vac. It is portable, which means it is easy to move and carry around.

The little Shop-Vac is nice for cleaning small spots. It also needs to be plugged in.

Emmett is about to open the little red Shop-Vac to empty it.

Inside you will find a filter and a place for all of the dirt and dust to go.

Here is a Bissell canister vacuum. It rolls around on the floor and is small.

With the push of a button the vacuum turns on. It also needs to be plugged in.

Here is another Hoover upright vacuum.

It is green and silver. It is also bagless.

A long cord and a hose attachment are included with the Hoover.

A button on the center of the vacuum will turn it on and off.

This Hoover also has bristles on the beater bar.

Emmett's favorite vacuum cleaner is called Henry. Henry has a smiling face. His nose is the hose of the vacuum.

Henry is a canister vacuum made in England by the Numatic International Company.

A long retractable cord is used to plug Henry in.

Henry has a dust bin that Emmett empties after he vacuums.

There is a lever to wind the cord up when Henry is done vacuuming.

This is a Dyson Ball vacuum cleaner.

It can turn a corner easily.

It is bagless.

A long red and grey extension hose are attached to the back of the Dyson Ball.

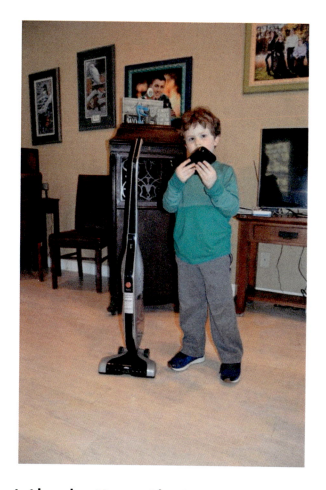

Look at the battery that powers this Hoover Cordless Lynx Stick Vacuum. Emmett will re-charge the battery when he is done vacuuming.

Once Emmett puts the battery into the vacuum, it will run.

The Hoover is light-weight and easy to push.

A small Dyson Ball vacuum cleans just like the big one, except it runs by a battery.

The yellow ball helps the vacuum to turn quickly and easily.

The red button will turn the Dyson on and off.

Which vacuum is your favorite?

The End

Dyson™, Hoover™, Eureka™, Numatic™, and Bissell™ are all registered trademarks.

Made in the USA
Las Vegas, NV
26 February 2023